BUNCHGRASS HISTORIAN   Volume 34, Numbers 2 & 3, 2008

EDITOR'S NOTE

This *Bunchgrass Historian* is a unique double issue containing one major article. This article on Colonel Steptoe's 1858 campaign was planned originally as a three-part article to be published in this 150th year of the commemoration of that campaign. It soon appeared the story would best be told in one major article.

The author intends this story to be readily accessible to the reader. He has written what might be termed literary non-fiction, using a literary form to make the story more compelling, exciting, and immediate to the reader. Thus, dialogue is introduced and indicated by italics rather than quotes, with quotes used only for actual quotations from the primary sources. Immersing himself in the primary sources and in the physical environment—his farm is near the route Steptoe took and he has walked most the terrain of the story—Mahlon has tried to imaginatively recreate the thoughts, feelings, and attitudes of those involved in this conflict.

ABOUT THE AUTHOR

Mahlon E. Kriebel was born on a family farm near Ladow Butte. Mahlon enjoyed a long career as a neurophysiologist, publishing 70 papers on electrophysiology of the heart and neurosecretion. He developed educational materials for chaos theory. He held guest positions at University of California, Irvine; University of Konstanz; University of Graz, and the Max Plank Institute, Göttingen. In 1985, he was named an Alexander von Humbolt scholar. After 35 years, Mahlon retired in 2002 as Professor in the Physiology Department at SUNY Health Science Center, Syracuse, NY. He then moved back to the family farm near Garfield.

COVER

Detail from a painting by Nona Hengen of the Parley of Col. Steptoe, Chief Vincent, and Father Joset. This painting fits the location of the third parley, which ended at Plaza. Used with permission of Nona Hengen and Richard Scheuerman.

TABLE OF CONTENTS

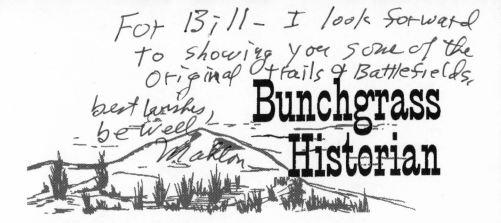

Bunchgrass Historian

Whitman County Historical Society
Colfax, Washington

Volume 34
Number 2&3
2008

Battle of To-hots-nim-me:
The U.S. Army vs. the Coeur d'Alene Indians
By Mahlon E. Kriebel

authorHOUSE®

AuthorHouse™
1663 Liberty Drive
Bloomington, IN 47403
www.authorhouse.com
Phone: 1-800-839-8640

Published by AuthorHouse   08/13/2012

ISBN: 978-1-4772-5529-2 (sc)
ISBN: 978-1-4772-5530-8 (e)

Library of Congress Control Number: 2012914026

Any people depicted in stock imagery provided by Thinkstock are models, and such images are being used for illustrative purposes only.
Certain stock imagery © Thinkstock.

This book is printed on acid-free paper.

A revised second edition of the **Bunchgrass Historian** *Vol. 34-2 & 3*

ACKNOWLEDGEMENTS

Special thanks to Ed Garretson for his encouragement, patience, and help in organizing the material. I am indebted to Father Thomas Connolly, S.J. for Coeur d' Alene Indian family histories, oral traditions, and for making suggestions in the manuscript in reference to Indian customs. Mary Ellen Trimble made valuable suggestions in early drafts. Donna Hanson introduced me to the National Archives where I found the original Kolecki Field Notes and Maps. Greg Partch shared his collection of B. Manring materials which were central in documenting Steptoe's condition of palsy. I thank Mrs. Randall A. Johnson for permitting the reproduction of her late husband's drawings. Nona Hengen allowed us to use her paintings for the covers. Michael Rule at the Turnbull National Wildlife Refuge provided maps and materials and showed us the area around Stubblefield Lake that fits the location of Seelah. Douglas Popwell II of the Washington State Department of Natural Resources kindly provided copies of 1870s survey maps that were invaluable in finding Indian trails. Special thanks to David Babb whose knowledge of Sanders Creek was invaluable in locating the Steptoe camp of May 16. The Coeur d' Alene Tribe gave permission to reproduce the 1840 Father Point portraits. Staff at the Washington State University and University of Idaho Library Archives helped find original materials. I thank Monika Kriebel for help in constructing dialogue. Thanks to Glenn Leitz and Steve Plucker for information and especially for hiking about the Palouse in quest of campsites and Indian trails.

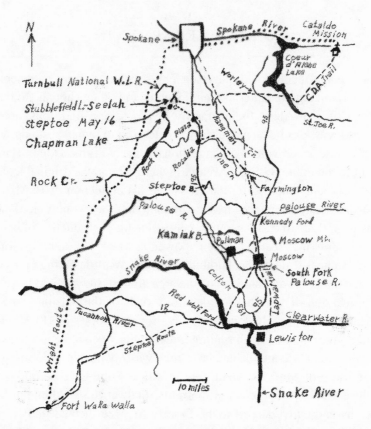

Map of Steptoe's Route. From Ft. Walla Walla, Steptoe followed an Indian Trail to Red Wolf Crossing (ford) at today's Timothy Park on the Snake River. Steptoe then followed Red Wolf Trail to the Lapwai Trail at Moscow (May 12 camp). He followed the Lapwai Trail N to cross the Palouse River at Kennedy Ford (May 13 camp). Steptoe continued on the Lapwai Trail to Pine Creek (May 14 camp near Farmington). He then followed Pine Creek for 15 miles to just S of Rosalia (May 15 camp). Steptoe next marched N 4 miles on a trail leading to Spokane. Then he turned NW onto a trail to Ft. Colville. He was stopped by Chief Vincent just S of Turnbull National Wildlife Refuge. The Indian encampment of Seelah (near Stubblefield Lake) is at the SE edge of the Refuge. Steptoe's May 16 camp was 3.6 miles SW of Seelah. The running battle of May 17 was between Plaza and Rosalia. The May 17 redoubt was located just S of Rosalia overlooking Pine Creek (at monument). The retreat route retraced their steps. Four months later, Wright marched on the direct trail from Ft. Walla Walla to Spokane House. The Battle of Four Lakes was just N of Turnbull Refuge. The Coeur d'Alene Trail from the Indian villages on the Coeur d' Alene River and Cataldo Mission went SW to the St. Joe River, then W, crossing the Lapwai Trail at Hangman Creek, and on to Seelah.

Battle of To-hots-nim-me:
The U.S. Army vs. the Coeur d'Alene Indians

By Mahlon E. Kriebel
Preface

The battle of To-hots-nim-me occurred on Coeur d'Alene land on May 17, 1858. It was a four-mile running battle that began at 8:00 am near Plaza, Washington, and ended 10 hours later on a hilltop in Rosalia. The 152 dragoons and seven officers under the command of Colonel Edward Steptoe were greatly outnumbered by Coeur d'Alene, Spokane, and Palouse warriors. At nightfall, with little ammunition left and 19 casualties, Steptoe and his men retreated to the Snake River. The army report states that the Indians had relaxed their vigilance, whereas Coeur d'Alene Indian oral tradition claims that the soldiers were allowed to escape. The battle was not planned by either side. Four months later, Colonel George Wright with a force of 700 soldiers ruthlessly punished the Coeur d'Alene, Palouse, and Spokane Indians by burning lodges, barns, and winter food stores, killing their horses, hanging Indians, and forcing them to sign treaties.

This recounting of the Battle of To-hots-nim-me [1] is based upon my extensive reading of the secondary literature and, after realizing the weaknesses of this literature, going to the primary sources. The contradictions and errors in the secondary accounts could not be corrected by referring to all authors so I have relied on only a few. I found it necessary to go to the primary sources to achieve my goal of a literary recreation of events as they may well have taken place and of locating these events on a modern map. The official reports, diaries, letters, reminiscences, surveys, and other documents I have studied are listed in the bibliography. I have used all available maps, and I have walked over the sites. I am indebted to members of the Coeur d'Alene tribe for their information and advice. From these I have reconstructed routes, battles, and campsites, and used words and described clothes for instance that were not actually recorded in any document. Thus the parleys between Vincent and Steptoe were reconstructed from Steptoe's, Gregg's, and Father Joset's accounts in the 35th Congressional Records and oral traditions published in *Saga of the Coeur d'Alene Indians* and *The Jesuits and the Indian Wars of the Northwest*. The trails and the actual locations were what brought the U. S. Army and Indians unexpectedly together. I have relied heavily on the

Drawing by Randall Johnson

original pencil and paper Field Note Maps by Theodor Kolecki, topographer on the Wright campaign. The May 16 army camp was 4 miles northwest of the traditional site and, since it was only 3½ miles from the Indian encampment of Seelah, its true position played a pivotal role leading to the running battle of May 17.

I: Steptoe's dragoons ride into a trap, May 16, 1858

In the fall of 1855, Colonel Edward J. Steptoe rode through the high desert region of the Great Basin, mapping a wagon route over the Snake Mountain Range. He had already marched over the military route from Fort Leavenworth, Nebraska, to the Great Salt Lake, then south to Cedar City, Utah Territory. The southwest assignment with dry, sweet air agreed with him and provided a much-needed respite from fatigue suffered in the Mexican-American War.[2]

Steptoe's Early Military Career: Steptoe was born in Virginia to a prominent family. His father was a physician, and his uncle was an influential judge who had recommended Steptoe's appointment to West Point with expectations that this career would make him into a man. Because of the Mexican-American War of 1846-1848, the army had to expand, and Steptoe rose in rank to brevet lieutenant colonel for gallant and meritorious conduct in the battles of Cerro Gordo and Chapultepec, where he commanded a new cavalry battalion referred to as "flying artillery." However, the pay scale lagged behind, which was a reason that Steptoe gave to postpone marriage. After the war, career officers looked west for deployment but were required to take a demotion in rank. Frontier duty was challenging as the U.S. Army was mapping the frontier, so Steptoe decided to remain in the military even though his turpentine business in Florida was paying handsomely.[3]

In 1855, President Franklin Pierce assigned Steptoe the investigation of the Gunnison Massacre. It had been alleged that Indians and members of the Church of Latter Day Saints (Mormons) had murdered pioneers near the Utah-Nevada border. Steptoe's diplomacy and attention to details exonerated the Mormons and held the Indians solely responsible. Because of Steptoe's success Pierce tendered the governorship of Utah Territory to Steptoe. Eastern papers endorsed Steptoe, and Congress quickly confirmed his appointment. Even though Steptoe and Pierce had developed a close friendship, Steptoe declined and suggested that Brigham Young, a Mormon, should be reappointed as governor.

Gov. Isaac Stevens
Drawing by Randall Johnson

Washington Territory and Governor Isaac Stevens: Lieutenant Isaac Stevens had resigned from the military in 1853 to accept the governorship of Washington Territory offered by President Martin Van Buren. Almost immediately Congress asked Stevens to search for a route for a railroad connecting Washington and Montana Territories. Stevens reported his explorations in *Route for the Pacific Railroad, near the 47th and 49th Parallels of North Latitude, from St. Paul, Min., to Puget Sound.* He found that the Palouse Prairie was crisscrossed by Indian trails.

Trails leading north from Fort Nez Perce at the confluence of the Walla Walla and Columbia Rivers to Colville and Spokane House crossed the Snake River at the mouths of the Palouse and Tucannon Rivers. A very good Nez Perce road, which had been used by Lewis and Clark, connected Fort Nez Perce to the confluence of the Clearwater and Snake Rivers. Stevens also used part of the Lapwai Trail between the South Fork of the Palouse River at Moscow and Lake Coeur d'Alene. A few miles downriver from present-day Lewiston was Red Wolf Crossing, which offered a ford on the Snake River. Red Wolf Trail led east to intersect the Lapwai Trail at Tahuna Hills (Paradise Ridge, Moscow). The Indian roads convinced Stevens that the Palouse Prairie was the gateway connecting Fort Nez Perce to Fort Benton on the Missouri River.

Colonel Edward J. Steptoe, from the Manring papers

Stevens hastily drafted treaties with Native Americans to permit frontier settlements west of the Columbia River. Since he held the posts of Governor, Commissioner for Indian Affairs for Washington Territory, and U.S. Army Surveyor, Stevens was able to intimidate the Indians to sign treaties during the Walla Walla Council at Fort Nez Perce in 1855. Stevens didn't care that each tribe was sovereign or that tribal boundaries existed. Many Indians later claimed coercion and rescinded their marks. The treaties were a complete failure. The implication of personal ownership and transfer of ceded lands to white settlers was not appreciated by Indians; they thought they could still use their ancestral lands even while living on a reservation. This misunderstanding was one reason for the Yakima Wars in 1855. The plateau tribes (Yakima, Wenatchees, Palouse, Klikatats, and others) lost and were forcibly moved onto reservations. Even though the Coeur d'Alene Indians controlled the routes over the Palouse Prairie and the Bitterroot Mountains to Fort Benton, they were not present at the treaty council. The Coeur d'Alene Indians were aware that their ancestral homelands were the gateway for east-west trade, so they formed alliances with neighbors (Kalispel, Spokane, and Flathead) to keep whites out.

Paradoxically, the military was charged to uphold rights of Native Americans as guaranteed by treaty while insuring safety for whites. Unfortunately, white miners had little regard for treaties because, from their perspective, the west seemed limitless and Indians had no written record of tribal boundaries. The white expansionism that was championed by Stevens was on a collision course with professional U.S. Army officers sympathetic to Indian rights, such as General John Wool, commander of the Pacific forces during the Plateau War. Information traveled quickly between Indian tribes and even over the Cascade Mountains because of alliances established through marriage and warfare. Consequently, the seeds of distrust had sprouted in the minds of the Coeur d'Alene Indians before Steptoe's incursion into the Palouse Prairie.

Both Steptoe and Stevens were West Point graduates. Even though Stevens was two classes ahead, they must have known each other at the academy since Stevens, who graduated first in his class, would have had major upper class duties. Both served in the Mexican-American War during the Battle of Cerro Gordo and the Battle of Chapultepec. By a strange twist of fate, the treaties drafted by Governor Stevens and his disrespect for Indian rights laid the groundwork for Steptoe's national humiliation after the retreat from the battle on the Palouse Prairie.

Steptoe's Command at Fort Walla Walla: Steptoe's early record showed that he was well suited to command a frontier fort. He had had experience with Indians in 1838, moving the Cherokee Nation to Oklahoma ("Trail of Tears"), and again in 1849 in Florida during the Seminole hostilities.[4] In 1856, Steptoe was assigned to Fort Vancouver, Washington, for frontier duty with orders to build Fort Walla Walla. The new fort was to be a departure depot during the construction of a military road to Montana.

Marching east from Portland in the fall of 1856, Steptoe experienced the dramatic change as the rain forest, where the Columbia River knifes through the Cascade Mountains, changes to the sand and sagebrush of the Central Columbia Plateau. Reaching the western steppes of the Blue Mountains, he must have marveled at the stamina and quickness of Umatilla Indian Cayuse ponies, which attested to the nutrient value of the fescue grass. The region was a cavalryman's dream, with wide open spaces and gentle hills carpeted with bunchgrass. The terrain offered exhilarating opportunities for maneuvers. Steptoe sent meticulous monthly "post returns" to Fort Vancouver that detailed building expenses and labor, as well as morale, sick rolls, and fort activities.[5] The "returns" show beautiful penmanship and attention to detail, indicating that Steptoe commanded respect and performance. At Fort Walla Walla, Steptoe appeared to be in good health; in a letter to his sister, he described how much he enjoyed prairie chicken hunting and stream fishing for trout.[6]

Courtesy of Library of Congress

Gustavus Sohon's drawing of Fort Walla Walla circa 1862.
The site was picked by Steptoe, and the first military buildings were constructed under his command.

In the 1850s, Washington Territory was in transition. Settlers were turning north from the Oregon Trail to plow the Walla Walla Valley to wheat even before treaties had been ratified by Congress. In defiance of Stevens' treaty of 1855, which restricted white settlement north of the Snake River and east of the Columbia River, miners had infiltrated the

TIMOTHY
FRIEND OF THE
WHITE MEN

Drawing by
Randall Johnson

mountains north of Spokane around Fort Colville. As expected, trouble erupted between whites and Indians. Initially, the army was sympathetic to the Indians. For example, in 1856, Stevens asked for army protection, which Colonel Wright declined because he thought that Stevens should stay out of Indian lands. Nevertheless, Steptoe sent a detachment from Fort Walla Walla to rescue Stevens and his entourage from an Indian attack.[7] Then, Major W.W. Mackall, Assistant Adjutant General, U.S. Army, San Francisco, ordered Steptoe to Fort Colville to calm prospectors and forge friendships with indigenous tribes. Steptoe anticipated cooperation from the Spokane and Coeur d'Alene Indians so that Lieutenant John Mullan's engineers could immediately begin building a road from Fort Walla Walla to Fort Benton, Montana. Steptoe apparently did not appreciate that this proposed army road, bisecting Coeur d'Alene Indian land, would be perceived by the Indians as an invasion.

Steptoe's March through Palouse Prairie: On May 6, 1858, Steptoe left Fort Walla Walla with three companies of dragoons (cavalry) and one mounted infantry company. It was a lovely spring morning and they marched leisurely northeast along the Walla Walla-Clearwater River Indian road toward the Snake River. The Nez Perce guides selected good camping spots spaced about 15 miles apart along clear streams flowing from the Blue Mountains. The column rode up the Pataha Valley, crossed the rolling hills of the Alpowa Divide, and descended along Alpowa Creek to Red Wolf Crossing on the Snake River (now Highway 12). In addition to his orders to march to Colville, Steptoe was looking for a band of Palouse Indians that had rustled a herd of cattle from Walla Walla. He and his men saw Indians, but the Indians were quick to keep the basalt breaks of the Snake River Canyon between them and Steptoe's troops.

During the descent to the Snake River, Steptoe appreciated why the Nez Perce Indian guides had picked this route. The Snake River Canyon twists and turns as it cuts through the Columbia Plateau. At many places the river was pinched between canyon walls into swirling caldrons and 10-foot standing waves. The river above and below the ford was a death trap for man and horse alike. At the junction of Alpowa Creek and Snake River Canyons, however, the surge of the Snake River dissipated over the broad gravel bars and formed a crossing. Chief Timothy's band of Nez Perce ferried the troops and swam the horses across the river without mishap. Red Wolf Crossing was a favorite Indian ford because a north rim canyon (Skalaisson's Ravine), Steptoe Canyon, lies almost opposite Alpowa Canyon on the south rim.

Source of the Palouse River. Engraving by Stanley after a drawing by Sohon. The basis for this print was a drawing by Sohon during a survey on the Lapwai Trail. Sohon mentioned climbing over a mountain before dropping down into the Palouse Valley. He made mention of a large butte to the west that would be Kamiak Butte. I propose that this view into the source of the Palouse is from Kamiak Butte. The mountain on the far right would be Moscow Mountain, the center peak in the distance is Mount Margaret, and far left mountain is Gold Hill. The view overlooks Kennedy Ford on the Palouse River. (From Steven's RR Survey)

On May 11, Steptoe's men rode single file along the narrow Red Wolf Trail, which jumped back and forth over the canyon creek for 5 miles until reaching the Palouse Plateau. The basalt bluffs were ablaze with yellow balsamroot interspersed with spikes of lavender lupine and clumps of pink phlox. They rode from the sagebrush of the lower canyon to the bunchgrass steppe about 1800 feet above the Snake River, where they saw spurs of the Bitterroot Range to the east.

Etienne Silmoulkelsimm, a powerful medicine man who converted to Christianity. He helped build the Cataldo Mission. Copy of an oil painting by Fr. Nicholes Point, S.J., done in the mid-1840s. Used by permission of the Coeur d'Alene Tribe.

Breaking camp on May 12, they continued on Red Wolf Trail in a northeasterly direction to the north-south Lapwai Trail and probably made camp north of Tahuna Hills (Paradise Ridge), where Governor Stevens had camped a few years earlier (South Fork of Palouse River, southeast of Moscow). Because of the leisurely pace, the condition of the cavalry horses improved with each passing day and the spirits of the enlisted infantry soared as they became saddle toughened.

On May 13, the column turned north on the Lapwai Trail and crossed over a mountain spur (western part of Moscow Mountain) before descending into the Palouse River Valley. The Palouse River was clear, with trout gorging on swarms of buffalo gnats and no-see-ums. The Lapwai Trail crossed the river at a gravel bed (Kennedy Ford) that had been used for millennia by bands of native peoples. The soldiers camped at the ford, where there was abundant grazing and firewood. According to a report by Lieutenant David Gregg, they were informed by Indians that they would be attacked if they didn't turn back. The troops discounted the warning.

Gustavus Sohon's drawing of the Mission at Cataldo, Idaho, 1858

Susan-Pick-Handle, a Coeur d'Alene who lived at the southern boundary of tribal lands near present-day Potlatch, was digging camas when she saw the column of soldiers leave the Palouse Valley on May 14. Mesmerized, she would probably have marveled at the organization of the horse soldiers as they fell into ranks. The column consisted of four companies of 152 enlisted men, 7 officers, 40 mule skinners driving 200 pack horses and cattle, 2 twelve-pound howitzers strapped to mules, and 2 gun carriages. The troops rode two abreast, spaced 20 feet apart, and were led by chief soldiers bearing flags. The dark blue coats with gold ropes (epaulets and shoulder scales), light blue trousers, and the array of caps and hats made a glorious serpentine of blue. Belt buckles and the single and double rows of brass buttons on the frock coats sparkled in the morning sun. She may well have wondered why a small band of Nez Perce warriors was riding up front, whereas a few Coeur d'Alene Indians mingled about the rear. Idle thoughts didn't fill her bag, so Susan-Pick-Handle returned to digging camas bulbs.

The column rode north, passing two valleys (Cedar Creek and Silver Creek) dotted with pools of water impounded by beaver dams before it reached the head waters of Ingossomen Creek (Pine Creek, at Farmington) for the campsite of May 14.[8] The following day, the troops left the Lapwai Trail, taking a minor trail leading northwest to Fort Colville via Spokane House. The cavalry rode northwest for 15 miles to camp on

May 15 along Ingossomen Creek (one half mile downstream from the trestle at Rosalia). They did not know that in two days they would form a redoubt on the hill immediately to their north after a running battle with Native Americans.

On May 16, the column left Ingossomen Creek, marched north for four miles on a trail that later became part of the Territorial Road, and then turned northwest (at Plaza) to cross a low watershed into a broad, gentle valley of Sanders Creek. The column continued along the valley for six miles before turning north (Wells Road and Sanders Creek) into a ravine winding between high hills. It was here that Steptoe and his men learned that they were "in a very dangerous place," as Indians were blocking the trail and hilltops were swarming with warriors. They had ridden into an ambush as they were about to leave the rolling Palouse Prairie and drop onto the flat scablands.

II: Indian Camas Encampment at Seelah

Spring Camas Encampment of Seelah: According to oral tradition, generations of Coeur d'Alene and Spokane Indians had camped in the region now known as the scablands in Eastern Washington to dig and roast camas bulbs, which served as a major food staple. Seelah, meaning "Granddad" and located near a small lake known as "Water Lily Lake," was one of the spring encampments.[9] This location offered a chance for the Coeur d'Alene People to escape the penetrating, cold grip of early spring in the panhandle of Idaho. Seelah was a place where many tribes of the Inland Northwest met to discuss events of winter and

Isidore Natathen, a Coeur d'Alene medicine man of great physical strength. He was an influential speaker for Christianity. Copy of an oil painting by Fr. Nicholas Point, S.J., done in the mid-1840s. Used with permission of the Coeur d'Alene Tribe.

strengthen family bonds. Camas was the reason the Indians were in the path of the U.S. Army.

Coeur d'Alene and Spokane Indians had traded peacefully with the Hudson's Bay Company since the late 1700s, and they readily accepted goods that made life easier. Many North American Indian villages had requested the Black Robes (Jesuits), and many Indians eagerly embraced Christianity as an aid in dealing with new technologies and plagues. By the 1850s, the era of slow generational change had passed. The rich grasslands of the Palouse Prairie were easily reached from Fort Walla Walla via Indian roads, and in the next 30 years the rolling Palouse Prairie was homesteaded and plowed to wheat.

Travel from the Coeur d'Alene Mission to Seelah: In the spring of 1858, several families from the Mission on the Coeur d'Alene River (Cataldo) made the trip to Seelah. Travel along the river required two crossings with canoes and the men swam the horses across. Mary rode Zachary's horse and he led his mother's mare. Even though infirm, she could still ride. Household gear was transported on travois. When the Palouse Tribe was digging with these Coeur d'Alenes eight years earlier, Zachary's mother had traded a bag of bitterroots for the horse. Six families from the Mission and Chief Vincent's band from Hayden Lake were joined by seven families living along the St. Joe River. They rode along the St. Joe River for 4 miles to a place where they could cross between two small lakes (Chatcolet and Hidden Lakes) to avoid the boggy ground south of the river. The men swam the horses across the 25-foot deep river, and women and children were ferried with canoes. This ford is pinched between the eastern rim of the plateau overlooking the St. Joe Valley and a mountain ridge to the east (near the bridge of a bike trail). After crossing, they camped at Hidden Lake.

The next day, about 15 families left for Seelah. The climb out of the St. Joe Valley followed a trail on top of a steep, narrow ridge that started at the shore of Lake Chatcolet and reached the prairie 1000 feet above within one-half mile. Generations of travelers had worn a deep path between red cedar and ponderosa pine trees (both path and original trees can be seen today east of Chatcolet Road, signed as Mullan Trail). Upon reaching the plateau they continued westward on the trail for about 5 miles before camping along Rock Creek a few miles east of present-day Worley. The trip had been made for generations, and the traditional campsites were spaced for reasonable travel days. Wright's troops would follow this road 5 months later after subjugating the Indians at Cataldo Mission.

The third leg of the trip wound through the rolling prairie to Nedwhauld on Lahtoo (Latah) Creek. Zachary's mother looked happier each day, especially after visiting with friends and relatives of the Spokane Tribe who were also en route to Seelah. The small band of Native Americans reached Seelah on day four. Families joined the encampment from Spokane, Colfax, and Tekoa, making 34 lodges. Every day the men drove the horses to pasture along a small creek (Sanders Creek). At night, the horses were picketed in the center of the compound.

Coeur d'Alene Indians at Seelah: Mary stirred, lifting Zachary's arm from the swelling of new life within her belly. She slid from the robes, threw her new blanket over her shoulders, and ducked under the lodge flap. Morning sunlight glowed red as it filtered through the frost-tipped grasses blanketing the hilltops. She gathered a few pine and aspen branches and poked them into the lodge, then swung the smoke flap wide open before ducking back inside. Stirring the fire pit, she placed pine twigs encrusted with pitch bubbles over embers that quickly ignited into a hot fire. Then she racked alder limbs over the fire pit and crawled back under the robes. The aspen burned cleanly, warming the inner walls of elk hides lining the tent poles. She felt secure next to Zachary. His mother sighed as she turned under her robes. Mary knew that the older woman was about to rise and would be thankful for the stoked fire.

After warming her cramped fingers by the fire, Mary's mother-in-law kneaded dried huckleberries gathered last fall into fresh camas mash to make cakes. The day before, roasted camas bulbs had been removed from the fire pit and mashed into a paste for "baking flour." The freshly dug camas was a welcomed respite from winter stores of camas loaves that were stale.

Preparing the fresh camas started with a roasting pit made by Zachary and Victor who lined a hole, ripped open by a wind-toppled tree, with rocks. A fire was made in the pit with aspen and cottonwood limbs. After the fire had died, the hot rocks were covered with willow branches, grass, and cow parsnip leaves. The camas bulbs were layered onto the leaves and then covered with a second layer of grass, leaves, and dirt. Women poured water along the edge until steam appeared, which signaled that the camas was cooking. The camas steamed for three days, during which time some of the starch changed to sugar. Freshly roasted camas is nutritious and tasty.

Camas digging was traditionally women's work. Zachary quietly helped out of respect for his mother, whose gnarled hands made chores difficult. After years of grubbing camas bulbs with a digging stick,

Drawing by Randall Johnson of the Butte that bears Steptoe's name

Zachary's mother was forced to watch as women and children pried the ping pong ball-sized bulbs from the marshy ground. A digging stick had a fire-hardened point with the other end fitted into a hole in a piece of elk antler. The women of Mary's family stuffed the brownish bulbs into corn husk bags. Mary treasured two made by her grandmother because the husks had been woven over kamiah twine (native hemp) gathered near Ingossomen Creek. The husks had been dyed in hot water with alder roots for green, sumac bark for orange, and oak bark for purple. Her grandmother taught her to weave but, being impatient, Mary had replaced native hemp with traders-cotton and used aniline dyes.

It must have felt wonderful to escape the cold confines of the villages hemmed between the Coeur d'Alene Mountains to Seelah, where spring arrives four weeks earlier. Working in the warm sun, the women had quickly filled their bags with plump and firm bulbs. They had arrived at Seelah at the right time, for in a few days the bulbs would expend their energy to produce the scape and flowers and become mushy. Immediately after gathering the bulbs, Mary had pounded some into a paste with a mortar and pestle that had been at this camas ground, in her grandmother's family for generations. Perhaps Mary then watched Zachary's mother as she sat on her heels cooking the cakes on a flat, hot rock of the fire ring.

Zachary was no doubt a good provider and his widowed mother always had elk meat and salmon. His mother had embraced the teachings of the Black Robes. Following Chief Vincent's lead, Zachary and Victor were also baptized. Many young men had enthusiastically helped the Jesuits build the new mission on the banks of the Coeur d'Alene River. The Priests had won the respect of the young men by felling the giant fir trees and hefting broad axes to hew timbers and posts. This was indeed men's work and Indians quickly learned to use the pit saw. They were naturals in rigging ropes and pulleys to set the huge post timbers for the corners of the mission.

Even with bow and arrow, Zachary and Victor were probably the best elk and deer hunters of all their people. They had spent the winter trapping beaver to trade at the Colville Hudson's Bay trading post in early spring. Zachary had traded the standard 10 pelts for a Hudson's Bay rifle and 6 for powder and lead. He then bartered 6 pelts for two 4-pelt blankets for his wife and mother. These highly prized blankets had 4 black stripes woven into the edge seams to indicate a worth of 4 beaver pelts. Since the traders seldom bested a Coeur d'Alene in barter, they had given them a name that meant "heart of a leather piercing awl." To Mary's surprise, Zachary also had presented her with a bolt of calico, which he had insisted on to close the deal. Zachary shot an elk shortly after they arrived at Seelah. Yes, she had a good husband.

Louise Siuwheem, sister of Stellaam and aunt of Chief Vincent. She was the driving force in the conversion of the Coeur d'Alene Indians to Catholicism. Copy of an oil painting by Fr. Nicholes Point, S.J., done in the mid-1840s. Used by permission of the Coeur d'Alene Tribe.

From this encampment at Seelah, Chief Vincent had sent warriors to meet the soldiers at the Palouse River to ask them to return to Fort Walla Walla. He had also instructed his scouts to count rifles and pistols. However, the soldiers ignored the warnings and continued on the Lapwai Trail for another 10 miles before camping at the headwaters of Ingossomen Creek (Pine Creek at Farmington). From this campsite Vincent hoped the troops would continue north on the Lapwai Trail and thus bypass Seelah. However, they had turned northwest to follow a trail leading directly to his people's encampment of Seelah. Last night the soldiers were only a morning's march away. The Coeur d'Alene Indians were not gathered for war but for visiting, digging camas, and gathering big-yoked duck eggs.

Chief Vincent's Heritage: Chief Vincent's father was a headman of the band at Hayden Lake, and his uncle, Joseph Stellaam, was the patriarch and war chief of the band living along the north shore of Coeur d'Alene Lake. Stellaam was a skillful stick game player and powerful medicine man. Consequently, it was natural that Vincent grew into a position of leadership. Traditionally, the Coeur d'Alene Tribe had jealously guarded its borders. It had prevented the Hudson's Bay Company from establishing a trading post, even though the Coeur d'Alene and St. Joseph valleys were teeming with beaver. Members did, however, trade at the posts established on neighboring lands. Vincent had jumped at the chance to obtain fishhooks with catgut leaders (early hooks were eyeless) imported from England.

When the first Jesuit mission by the St. Joseph River flooded, the priests moved to a hill overlooking the flood plain of the Coeur d'Alene River and built an impressive, baroque wooden church (Cataldo). Stellaam tolerated the Black Robes, but perhaps his love for gambling, which was discouraged by the priests, was his reason for rejecting Catholicism. Surprisingly he did not object to his wife's conversion. This dualism indicates that the Coeur d'Alene People highly regarded independent thinking and personal rights. Vincent's mother Martha was an early convert and presumably had a powerful influence on her son, who had been baptized by Father Joset. Vincent's second wife, Anna Monica, was a prominent, enthusiastic Catholic. Vincent was a devoted father and had a daughter with each wife.

Chief Vincent's Worst Fear: *Chief Vincent bolted upright, tugged on his buckskin shirt which clung to his chest dripping with cold sweat. Horses were galloping past his tent, men whooping, women screaming and guns firing. His worst fear of a sneak attack was happening:* a repeat of

1856 when the Washington Territorial Volunteers under the command of Benjamin Shaw had slaughtered an encampment of Walla Walla, Cayuse, and Palouse Indians digging camas in the Grande Ronde Valley. Shaw had caught the Indians in open space. The slaughter continued all afternoon as the Volunteers hunted those attempting to hide in the willows. Sixty women, children, and old men were slain.[10] News of the massacre had spread like a prairie fire throughout the northwest.

Now it was happening again. Vincent, thinking he had made a ghastly mistake by not taking the initiative, grabbed his rifle and ducked under the tent flap. Perfect timing for an attack as night was giving way to pink skies and most people were still asleep. The raid was swift. Soldiers toppled tepees which ignited with embers left from night fires. People were running every which way, a mother was clubbed and her child fell under a charging horse. Within seconds, the raid was over. Half dressed men, women, and children lay dead, others milled about, blood soaking through shirts and dresses as they searched for family. Indian horses had been shot or scattered.

Vincent rose from a troubled sleep. His lodge was dark, silent. He had had a dream. Slipping from the tepee so as not to waken his wife, Anna Monica, his mother Martha, and his daughter, he grabbed the braided hackamore and horse blanket by the tent flap. Stroking the horses picketed in the center of the encampment he quietly moved to his treasured white Cayuse mustang. Walking his horse he startled a couple dogs who whined as they followed along. The encampment of Seelah slept. Red clouds blanketed the expanse of green hills as he rode south from "Water Lily Lake" (Stubblefield Lake) towards the horse soldier's camp at Ingossomen Creek.

Reaching a gentle, wide valley (Sanders Creek), Vincent turned easterly into the rising sun. He knew this trail well. In a few miles it would join a major intersection of trails that fanned across the rolling prairie, connecting tribal families living to the south and east on the Palouse River. *Vincent recalled events pertaining to the advancing soldiers in an effort to understand their mission. Were they on a warpath? What had the Coeur d'Alene Indians done to provoke war? Or, could this be a peaceful mission? But then, the cavalry hadn't sent runners in advance to ask for permission to ride through Coeur d'Alene Lands.*

Sunrise, May 16, 1858: Vincent had sent a runner to request a visit from Father Joset to insure peace. Joset was from Switzerland and fluent in several languages. He had readily learned the difficult Coeur d'Alene language and basic customs, which explains his success in teaching and converting Indians to Christianity. As Vincent continued toward Ingossomen Creek, the sun was casting shadows from the hilltops into the valley. *His mind raced with questions. Had his judgment failed?* On May 14 during Chief Andrew Seltice's annual barbecue near Liberty Lake, Chief Vincent had argued passionately that the Coeur d'Alene People must prevent the soldiers from entering their ancestral lands. Chief Seltice counseled that they should *lay down your arms and go meet Steptoe in friendship . . . he will go around our country . . . We are not yet in battle with Steptoe, and battle can still be avoided by friendly talk.* Vincent had argued *it is now too late for any dodging around. Steptoe has already crossed the Snake River and is coming directly towards our villages.* Many warriors, especially the subchief Malkapsi, wanted to fight immediately, but Vincent, who had wisely led for 14 years, prevailed with his council to first find out the soldiers' mission. If reason did not convince the soldiers to return, then they would force them to return. Father Joset had always preached peace because there were so many whites in America and Europe that it was inevitable that they would settle the west. Vincent needed Joset's council to reaffirm that it would be impossible to win a prolonged war against so many whites. Since many of the warriors had converted, Father Joset would calm raw feelings. Moreover, because Joset was not an American, many Indians trusted his judgment.

Vincent had ridden about 8 miles when he spied the soldiers. His heart sank as he watched the column turn from the main trail (one mile south of Plaza) onto the trail to Seelah. Strange, the troops didn't seem to be in a hurry, and the Nez Perce guides were riding along with the soldiers. The relaxed pace didn't indicate a war party. Riding hard back to Seelah and thinking of the Grande Ronde Massacre, rage seized his chest as he realized that the Nez Perce scouts were leading the soldiers to Seelah!

Vincent stopped at the edge of the rolling prairie overlooking Seelah. It was a pastoral sight of blue fields with the array of white tepees silhouetted against cottonwoods. Surveying the trail dropping from the hills onto the flat scrabble land of his encampment, *the war chief thought that his warriors could either intimidate the soldiers from the hilltops to retreat or fight long enough to allow their families to escape into the forests.*

Within minutes Vincent reached the village. He called for his brother-in-law Zachary and Victor, an important headman with good sense. Even though young, both were already influential men. In the meantime, Chief Sgalgalt of the Spokane Tribe had arrived with warriors. They all agreed that the soldiers were on a war mission. Vincent insisted that they should parley with the soldiers before combat. As the camp sprang to life, the chiefs rode back to the defensible hilltops.

For the soldiers, mornings had become routine and days uneventful. The morning of May 16, Captain Charles S. Winder had no reason to suspect that the tenth day of their march through the Palouse Prairie would be different. After grazing the horses, the men quickly fell into ranks and proceeded along the trail to Fort Colville. They marched along a small creek (North Fork of Pine Creek) for two miles, then turned northwest onto a little-used Indian trail to cross over a low watershed into

BATTLE SCAR

THIRD MODEL, DRAGOON

Colt Revolver

CAL. 45

a gentle valley (Sanders Creek, Wentworth Road). The horses were in wonderful condition, and the men rode easily for 6 miles before turning north from the valley to follow the trail winding between high hills.

At first, the army scouts did not see the chiefs, who were obscured by a bend in the ravine. Finally, about noon, the scouts noticed the chiefs 400 yards ahead and immediately stopped. Soon hundreds of warriors appeared on the hilltops. A contingency of Coeur d'Alene and Spokane Indians dressed in splendid shirts and trousers rode toward the column, then stopped. After a minute, Steptoe, flanked by soldiers bearing flags, rode forward. Vincent and Sgalgalt remained motionless. The cool spring air blanketing the valley didn't convey the mounting tension. *Vincent admired Steptoe as he rode up the ravine, making an easy target.*

III Collision

Vincent Meets Steptoe, First Parley, noon, May 16: Two accomplished, respected, and confident men signaled a guarded acknowledgement. Both were scions of prominent families with influential uncles. Both were sons of successful men. Both were born of women of prestige. Both were devoted to family. Both were clear thinkers and skilled diplomats. Both had proven their courage. Both were deeply spiritual and religious. Both were avid trout fisherman.

Drawing by Randall Johnson

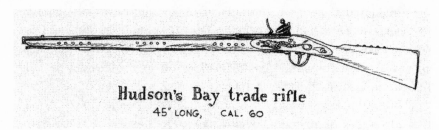

Tragically—both belonged to cultures on a collision course.

Chief Vincent wore his finest smoked-buckskin war shirt and leggings made of scraped elk hide. The seams were feathered, making a soft outline. The beaded blue shoulder straps with bold tribal floral designs sparkled. Beautifully beaded gauntlets matched his moccasins. The beadwork was a testament to the artistic skills of his wife. His war bonnet supported 24 rabbit-hair-tipped eagle feathers; the quill of each was wrapped with red yarn to anchor the feather to the beaded head strap. Eight ermine tails dangled from brass beads threaded to each side of the bonnet. Vincent's breastplate of bone dowels, made from the fibulas of 40 deer and hundreds of brass beads, indicated that he was a valiant warrior. His rifle was sheathed in a beaded scabbard of moose hide. It was comfortably cradled in his arm. He sat on his treasured Navajo chief blanket. He had traded a corn husk bag for the black and white striped blanket with red bars of hand-spun yarn with an Indian at Fort Nez Perce. Vincent and horse were as one.

Steptoe wore a faded dark blue coat with epaulets indicating his rank. His coat supported two rows of brass buttons. His light blue trousers showed neatly-sewn tears from the thorny ocotillo of the southwest desert. The brim of his officer's hat was pulled low to shield his large, dark, penetrating eyes and temples that were exposed by a receding hair line. Feathers of a prairie hen that he had shot at Fort Walla Walla were tucked under his hat cord. Last night, Steptoe had repaired some split seams on his boots and polished them. A colt revolver and sword hung from his belt, which was secured with a brass buckle stamped "U.S. Army." A large, well-trimmed handlebar mustache and prominent sideburns hid much of Steptoe's delicate face. He carried himself with confidence and sat comfortably on the padded Grimsley saddle.

Vincent first addressed Steptoe in Coeur d'Alene, and Steptoe answered in English. Then, in Canadian voyageurs French, Vincent asked why the troops were marching through Coeur d'Alene territory. Spoken French surprised the officer and his face relaxed. In high school Parisian French, Steptoe answered that he was on a peace keeping mission to Fort Colville. Both men realized that their French was not all that compatible. They would need the Nez Perce scouts for interpreters. Steptoe motioned for his scouts to join him.

Chief Vincent bristled at the sight of the Nez Perce but realized that they were necessary. For generations, the 8000-strong Nez Perce Nation had treated the Coeur d'Alenes poorly. With ten times as many warriors, the Nez Perce were always trying to start a fight. Nevertheless, a band of Nez Perce would always send a runner ahead to ask permission to ride through Coeur d'Alene lands. Yet this time neither the army horse soldiers nor the Nez Perce had sent a runner asking permission. Vincent could only conclude that the horse soldiers were spoiling for a fight. In light of the Stevens treaty council, Vincent could expect that the Nez Perce scouts would side with the whites and probably twist his questions to their advantage. But Vincent had no other choice. However, with Coeur d'Alene and Spokane warriors gathering on the hilltops, the Nez Perce thought better than to commit treachery at this moment. Vincent repeated his question in Coeur d'Alene. The Nez Perce scouts translated into English. Steptoe responded in English, which was translated into Coeur d'Alene. The conversation matched the preceding one in French.

Steptoe calmly stated: *I am Colonel Steptoe. We are marching to Fort Colville and ask the Spokane Indians to help us cross the Spokane River with canoes.*

Not able to suppress his anger, Vincent replied: *You are not on Spokane land. This is Coeur d'Alene Land. I am Coeur d'Alene.* Vincent, while pointing to the west, continued: *If you are traveling to Fort Colville why did you not travel to the west of here on the direct trail to Fort Colville? You should have crossed the Snake River at the Tucannon River and marched north along Sil-say-poo-west-tsin Lake (Rock Lake)!*

Not referring to his field order to engage the Palouse Indians, Steptoe calmly replied: *We thought that the water was too high in the Snake River to cross at the Tucannon River, so we marched up the Pataha Valley, then down Alpowa Canyon to Red Wolf Crossing on the Snake. As you know, this is a safe ford during the spring run-off.*

Chief Sgalgalt of the Spokanes stated: *You must turn back.*

Steptoe smiled, mustered a relaxed manner, and repeated his request: *Will you help us cross the Spokane River with canoes?* The Indian's demeanor didn't change.

Chief Sgalgalt curtly replied: *No, we Spokanes will not provide canoes.*

Vincent continued to press: *Did you not know that you are trespassing?*

Steptoe decided to try another tack. *He thought that his 152 soldiers and 7 officers, as well as the 30 packers and 10 Nez Perce guides, would intimidate the Coeur d'Alenes, who could muster no more than 75 warriors, to submit.* He stated: *We thought that the Coeur d'Alenes were our friends. May we proceed to the Spokane River?* His facade was eroding as more warriors were blanketing the hilltops. Steptoe thought, *where did all these Indians come from?* He was not aware that the Coeur d'Alenes, Kalispells, Pend Oreilles, Flatheads, and Spokanes had pledged to keep the army out of their lands.

Vincent waited for a reply to his question. The Nez Perce scouts looked to bolt.

Steptoe's mind raced: *of course he knew where he was. After all he was skilled in topography. Moreover, he recognized he was in sovereign Indian land. Sensing that his mission was in jeopardy and that the chiefs would not yield, Steptoe knew he needed time to save his mission. He couldn't trust his scouts.* Steptoe replied: *the Americans only want peace; I am an emissary of good will.* Steptoe was not aware that in 2 miles the trail passed through Seelah and that, consequently, his statement of peace appeared disingenuous.

Vincent could see that Steptoe's demeanor had changed. Nevertheless, he admired his diplomacy and answered: *If you are on a peace mission, why have you marched with so many armed soldiers? Your mules carry two guns that speak twice. You have a long pack train with many supplies. We think that your mission is to destroy us.* Vincent realized he had the advantage: *You can either fight us now or turn back.*

Steptoe had to accept the chiefs' resolve. *He was keenly aware of the war paint on both warriors and horses. Since the warriors were only hollering and shouting, Vincent was obviously in control. It was now clear to both men that Vincent held Steptoe's fate with a gesture of his arm.* With his façade fading, Steptoe replied: *I have no ill feelings towards the Coeur d'Alene and Spokane Indians.*

Steptoe looked to the hilltops. If his column continued in the ravine, his men would be helpless as they were easy targets. His face drawn, he continued: *We do not wish to fight and we will turn back.*

Steptoe wheeled his mount, mustering all his mettle, and with a stiff spine he slowly rode back to his men. His column was flanked by warriors taunting and rudely gesturing.

Steptoe thought: *This is a very dangerous place and we could be cut to pieces any second.* His troops had tightly closed ranks. The young recruits looked frail, the column small against the expanse of the rolling prairie as far as the eye could see. Riding to the rear, Steptoe addressed Gregg: *We may have to fight our way out of here, prepare your men.*

The trail to this "dangerous place" in Sanders Creek valley had no defensible positions, so Steptoe decided to ride to the southwest in search of one. The bugle sounded a retreat and the dragoons rode out of the ravine into the unknown.

During the retreat, Indian warriors charged to within pistol range, attempting to provoke a fight. The soldiers were scared but maintained rank and were determined "not to fire the first gun." Providence was with the soldiers. "After riding a mile," as Gregg noted, they rode through a "sheet of water" and gained a small hill a few yards from the rim of a bluff above a small creek (Sanders Creek). The column closed ranks, mounted side by side, and formed a 300-yard defensive line looking over the skiff of water. The cliff protected their back side. The pack horses were positioned between the rim of the bluff and the line of cavalry. The Indians continued to charge and taunt but stopped just out of range on the other side of the "sheet of water."

For the moment, Steptoe had gained time to think. He had only two options. If he aborted his mission, Mullan would not be able to enter these lands with a road-building crew and Steptoe would be perceived as a coward. On the other hand, if he stayed to fight, his column would surely be annihilated.

Chiefs Vincent and Sgalgalt watched in disbelief as the soldiers left the trail and rode to the canyon rim to take a defensive position only three miles from Seelah. Shaken, Vincent addressed his entourage: *Today is Sunday; I think that the horse soldiers will fight tomorrow.*

The Second Parley, Afternoon, May 16: Noting that the soldiers had gained a defensible position, Chief Sgalgalt of the Spokane and Chief Vincent of the Coeur d'Alene Tribes concluded that they must ride into Steptoe's camp for another parley in order to avert battle. As Steptoe watched the chiefs riding towards his redoubt, he surely thought that they were brave men. Steptoe rode toward them for a second parley. The chiefs explained that since it was still early afternoon, they believed the soldiers wanted to fight the next day or else they would be retracing their steps toward Ingossomen Creek.

The parley turned into a three-hour confrontation. Warriors charged and taunted. The soldiers remained "on frontal guard." It was a

Father Joset
JESUIT MISSIONARY,
CATALDO

Drawing by Randall Johnson

face-off. Steptoe argued that his men were very tired and simply couldn't continue. *Vincent noted that Steptoe was having trouble staying in his saddle and was beginning to tremble.* The stress had induced another ischemic attack[11] in which swelling within his skull caused a pounding headache, disrupted his motor cortex, and impaired cognitive function.

Vincent told Steptoe that by tomorrow there would be many more warriors who wished to fight. Vincent suggested that, if Steptoe retreated and left his supplies, packhorses, and cattle, his warriors would accept his retreat as a victory and not fight. Steptoe argued that he couldn't leave his supplies. Vincent stated that Steptoe had no choice. Several variations of an acceptable retreat were offered by Steptoe. However, Vincent stood fast: if there were to be no fight, the Indians must receive the supplies as battle booty. I propose that Steptoe; looking extremely haggard and making no sense, submitted and accepted the terms for peace by agreeing to leave the supplies.

Vincent, Zachary, Victor, and Sgalgalt rode back to their warriors. Even though many warriors preferred to fight, they agreed most reluctantly to accept the supplies as battle booty. Malkapsi, the tribal hothead, screamed for war, but did not win over the chiefs.

Nightfall, May 16: The dragoons had remained mounted for three hours. Indians continued to ride to the "sheet of water," just out of range. Others prowled in the underbrush along Sanders Creek below the canyon rim, preventing troops from watering horses. Finally, at dusk, the warriors retreated to the hilltops and the chiefs to Seelah.

Lt. David McM. Gregg, from the Manring papers

As nightfall approached, the soldiers dismounted, watered their horses, and made camp. Captain Charles S. Winder was officer of the day and posted heavy guards. Surprisingly, a Palouse Indian courier arrived from Fort Walla Walla with a dispatch and a letter to Winder. The Indian, Wyecat, was ordered back with a letter to Lieutenant Dent explaining Steptoe's plight. [Even though Wyecat managed to slip past the warriors and deliver the message, he was later hung for earlier mischief by Wright.] Upon receipt of the dispatch, Dent set out the following day with supplies and met Steptoe's retreating men on May 19 at the Snake River.

The men took turns allowing their mounts to forage. Steptoe and his officers presumably discussed their situation. Their small hill offered some defense, with the rim of the canyon protecting them from the west and the shallow skiff of water offering some protection to the east. However, the Indians would have the rising sun to their backs for a morning attack.

Knowing that their lives would depend on their mounts in the morning, soldiers would have spent the next hour drying and brushing their horses, picking out dirt and stones lodged between frog and horse shoe. The farrier, Elijah R. Birch who was later wounded, would have tightened any loose shoe. Like soldiers, horses had to eat each morning and night. After grazing their horses for an hour, the soldiers would have taken turns leading their mounts down a trail to the creek. Horses have very good night vision and were accustomed to their masters stumbling alongside. The cool water was a respite for parched throats.

After tending to their horses, men would have spent the night checking equipment. The latigo used to cinch the saddle was particularly prone to wear. Each soldier carried spare buckles, a spare horseshoe tucked in a compartment of the saddle, scraps of leather, and punches for general maintenance. Anticipating the possibility of a running battle, the light artillery soldiers would have greased the axles and tightened the felloes and spokes of the canon carriage wheels by wrapping them with water-soaked burlap.

The dragoons would have cleaned their 70-caliber U.S. musketoons. These were loaded with a ramrod and fired with a percussion cap. They were heavy and only effective at close range. Gregg's dragoons had new breech-loading Sharps carbines with a range of 400 yards. The single-shot dragoon pistol was holstered from the saddle horn and was effective only at close horse-to-horse combat. The officers had 45-caliber Colt revolvers, which provided good firepower because the cylinder held 6 rounds. However, each cylinder was loaded through the barrel with a ramrod and this took time. For close combat skirmishes, sabers would have been effective, but only the officers had brought theirs.

Meanwhile, bone tired after his 54-mile ride that started May 15 from the mission, Father Joset had arrived at Seelah. Five months later, Mullan noted the distance between Cataldo and Seelah was 54 miles.

Joset stated he rode 90 miles. I believe he meant 90 kilometers. This is significant because Joset also stated that Seelah was "6 miles" from the soldiers' camp of May 16. Seelah to the Sanders Creek camp is 3.6 miles or 6 kilometers. I posit that Joset meant kilometers; the confusion may have come out in the translation of Joset's French account into English. He later complained that he had been unable to sleep because he could hear warriors singing and drumming from the hilltops surrounding the army redoubt.

The night of May 16, 1858, Lieutenant Gregg did not know he would return to the battle field of May 17 to gather the bones of men he talked with that night about their fears of death. For 7 soldiers and 3 Nez Perce scouts, this was the last night. Captain Oliver H. P. Taylor, who had a wife and two little girls at Fort Walla Walla, and Lieutenant William Gaston were assigned to the flanks during retreat; this was their last assignment. Sergeant William C. Williams might have offered encouragement to the green recruits Charles H. Harnish, Victor C. DeMoy,

Lt. William Gaston, from the Manring papers

and James Crozet, who had not yet experienced battle. At Fort Walla Walla the recruits had been full of bravado. Now, they were lost in a sea of hills, and Steptoe and his officers had decided to retreat. *Gaston, feeling the growing lump in his throat, surely thought that the coming morning, with sunrise behind Indian lines, could be his chance for immortality. Would he return fire to end the truce?*

This spring, I returned to the May 16 redoubt at dusk. I stood on the small loess hill and felt a connection with Steptoe and his troops. I thought of the dragoons, mounted and maintaining ranks on the narrow hill for three hours. Both men and horses must have desperately needed water. Yet Sanders Creek was only 100 yards to the west at the base of the bluff! Looking to the east, I wondered if the two canons were positioned to fire to the right and left of the "sheet of water." Winder was Officer of the Day. Where had he posted sentries? Jerky was chewed, but I wager not swallowed, as fear no doubt gripped each man. I doubt if anyone slept.

Third Parley, Early Morning, May 17: By early morning the hilltops were quiet. Reveille was at 2:00 a.m. Horses and cattle were watered; men ate hardtack (biscuits) while their mounts snatched a few mouthfuls of bunchgrass. The pack animals were loaded. The cavalry broke camp at daylight and marched east for 2 miles to regain the trail back to Ingossomen Creek.

Three and an half miles to the north, at Seelah, Father Joset rose. He had had a fitful night and was still weary after his two-day ride. He counseled Chief Vincent not to engage in war because the U.S. would ultimately fight a war of extermination. According to Joset, he and Vincent decided to ride to the redoubt for a third parley to insure peace, but they found the redoubt vacated. Riding hard, Joset overtook the column alone to broker the third parley. Steptoe bluffed that he couldn't stop his column because the pack animals were excited. Steptoe didn't want to give the Indians time to set up an ambush, so he agreed to parley while marching. Catching up to the head of the column as it rode out of Sanders Creek valley (Wentworth Road) at about 7 a.m., Vincent and Joset rode to Steptoe's side.

Vincent: *As you can see, we meet again in peace.*

Steptoe reaffirmed that he had no intention to fight and would continue to Fort Walla Walla. Warriors were now appearing on hilltops, and Steptoe ordered his dragoons to hold fire. Suddenly, a Nez Perce guide struck Chief Vincent with his horsewhip and insulted him with the famous quote: *Proud man, why do you not fire?* Demonstrating that it was the Nez Perce who wished combat and not the soldiers, Steptoe immediately reprimanded the scout. The situation was defused. Victor stated, *There is nothing more to do here, let us each return to his home.*

Capt. Oliver H. P. Taylor, from the Manring papers

The Running Battle, May 17, 1858: Many Coeur d'Alene Indians watched the retreat of the soldiers from hilltops and were well aware that Father

Joset and Chief Vincent had marched with Colonel Steptoe to insure a safe retreat. Joset recounted that while Vincent was talking to Steptoe, Vincent's uncle rode up to warn them that the Palouses were planning to fire upon the column. Jean-Pierre, also a chief, stated he supported the proposition of Victor. Then Malkapsi became furious and slapped Jean-Pierre and hit Victor with his whip handle. The diminutive priest seized the "infuriated man" and actually calmed him. Thereafter the soldiers turned into a narrow valley leading to the North Fork of Pine Creek (one mile south of Plaza). Shortly before reaching the canyon of North Pine Creek, some Palouse warriors ambushed the column. For two miles firing was sporadic, and there were no casualties. The soldiers did not return fire until crossing the North Fork of Pine Creek about 400 yards north of a basalt mesa, where, as Gregg commented, they became "warmly engaged." Seeing the Indians riding to take possession of the first hill to the south, Gregg was ordered to take the hill. After gaining the first hill, Winder set his cannons. Gregg then raced the Indians for control of the hill one mile southeast of the first hill, which he secured. At this stage, the three dragoon companies were each separated by 1000 yards.

The Coeur d'Alene Indians watched Gregg's company leave the main body of soldiers from a hilltop to the east. Thinking that the Coeur d'Alenes should join the battle, Malkapsi continued to agitate and cajole the Coeur d'Alene warriors to fight. Standing nearby, Malkapsi's parents chided him, saying the soldiers were his enemies, these were his friends! Malkapsi, both rebuked and ashamed, replied *Oh, well, let us go and die.*

U.S. MOUNTAIN HOWITZER
6 POUNDER

Drawing by Randall Johnson

About a dozen, including Zachary, Jacques, Victor along with a group of Spokanes followed Malkapsi into the ravine which separated Gregg's dragoons from the main body of soldiers. Oral tradition tells that the Coeur d'Alene Indians thought they could "cut the head of the snake from the body" by positioning themselves in the ravine between the two hills to "be close to the next company when it rode from the first hill."

Gregg, however, observed that the Indians had ridden into the ravine in order to ambush Gaston's company as it broke over the hill. When Gregg saw Gaston beginning his charge down the slope of the hill, Gregg ordered his company to wheel and charge back into the ravine. The two companies passed at a right angle in a scissor maneuver, trapping the Indians. The Indians panicked, fired too quickly, and missed. They had fast, nimble ponies, but they were surprised at how rapidly the noose closed. The heavier dragoon horses pushed the Indian ponies into a tight clot against the basalt wall of the ravine. The soldiers fired point blank. Within seconds, about twelve Indians were killed, including Zachary, Vincent's nephew, and Jacques. Victor was mortally wounded. There were no soldier casualties during this skirmish. The two dragoon companies wheeled, stopped, and reloaded. At this moment, Victor was dragged to safety and other warriors recovered the bodies of Zachary and Jacques. Jacques was later buried at the battlefield.

Lieutenant Lawrence Kip, from the Manring papers

Mary had heard the faint reports of guns and knew when she saw Malkapsi with a fallen brave that her husband was dead. Father Joset, with a heavy heart, buried Zachary at Seelah. The Indians returned to the Mission. Victor died en route and was buried near the Mission; his son carried his name. Mary later named her newborn Zachary.

The battle ravine is south of the hill that currently has an airstrip (two miles north of Rosalia), and most of the Indian casualties took place here. In fall 2008, a group sponsored by the Whitman County Historical Society went on an excursion following Steptoe's trail. We stopped and walked up the road in the ravine (200 yards east of Pine Creek, on the Washington Territorial Road). Merle SiJohn, a descendent of Victor, gave a moving prayer.

The battle continues: After the skirmish, the three companies and artillery attachment gathered together where the ravine opens into Pine Creek Valley. Gaston's company rode along the east flank and Taylor's rode along Pine Creek to protect the west flank. After riding one half mile (3,300 feet from ravine), Taylor was mortally wounded with a shot to his neck. Gaston was shot through his body while securing the third hilltop (8,300 feet south of the ravine and 2,600 feet east of Pine Creek). His dragoons panicked and rejoined the main column. They left Gaston to die where he fell. Four months later, a Coeur d'Alene Indian led Lieutenant Mullan to the site to collect Gaston's remains. The Coeur d'Alene Indian related that he had buried Gaston. However, poor Gaston's bones had been scattered by wolves and his skull was not found. His saber was made into a knife.

After Gaston and Taylor were shot from their horses, the column continued along Pine Creek for another mile until it reached a long north-south lying hill where the soldiers established a redoubt (site of present monument) overlooking Pine Creek and their campsite of May 15. Taylor died at the redoubt. The men formed a circle with pack animals, cattle, and supplies protected in the middle. One field piece was positioned to fire to the north and the second was positioned to fire to the south. There were many skirmishes, but the redoubt provided protection against two frontal assaults although as Steptoe reported "the wounded increased in number continually." Nevertheless, the Indians did not mount a determined attack during the waning hours of sunlight. Chief Vincent was War Chief and insisted that the Indians halt their evening attack. The Spokane Indians held the hill to the north, and the Palouse Indians were positioned to the west with Pine Creek between them and the army redoubt. The Coeur d'Alene Indians held the hills to the east and perhaps the south. At this time, casualties were about equal on each side. The army suffered two officers, five enlisted men, and three Nez Perce scouts killed. Indians later admitted to 12 killed, including the three Coeur d'Alene sub-chiefs, Victor, Zachary, and Jacques. The Indians could not have known that the soldiers had only three rounds of ammunition each.

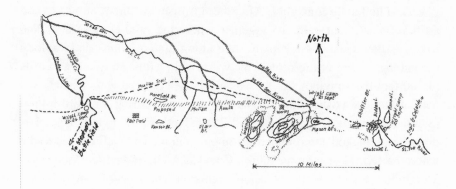

Proposed Coeur d' Alene Trail from St. Joe River to Latah Creek (Nedwhauld)

The Mullan Reconnaissance Map was traced and enlarged to overlay features of the St. Maries 30 x 60 minute topography map. Both maps were anchored together at the prominent bend of Latah Creek and the ridge that descends from the plateau to the St. Joe River between Chatcolet and Hidden Lakes. Mullan indicated rivers, creeks, mountains, and lakes with such accuracy that locations were readily identified. Hidden, Chatcolet and Round Lakes are presently joined since the level of Coeur d'Alene Lake was raised. The trail crossed between Chatcolet and Hidden Lakes at the bridge causeway. The Mullan Map indicated Warners Mt., Worley Mt, Mason Butte, and Shoeffler Butte with concentric circles that I have matched on the topography map with concentric hatch marks. I have sketched the course of Latah Creek and Rock Creek with its tributaries from both the Mullan Map and topography map. Note that Mullan placed Rock Creek and its tributaries too far north. Thus, the Mullan Trail indicated on the Reconnaissance Map bends too far north. However, when the route is adjusted to cross the tributaries of Rock Creek as indicated on the Mullan Reconnaissance Map to the topography map, the Coeur d' Alene Indian Trail went in a straight line from Worley to Latah Creek and passed just to the north of Morefield Butte. Wright's camp of September 20, which was just east of the St. Joe River, would now be underwater, near the bike bridge. The Wright camp of September 21 was on Rock Creek about three miles east of Worley. Wright's camp from September 22-26 is just south of the bridge of the Kentucky Trail Road.

Initially, Steptoe decided to remain and fight the next morning, but after conferring with his officers, he agreed to "run the gauntlet" under cover of night in the hope that some would reach safety. The soldiers buried their dead and the two cannons. First Sergeant Edward Ball was ordered to pour out the brandy stores. He emptied too much into his stomach and passed out under a clump of bushes, where he remained undetected the next morning. He later walked back to Fort Walla Walla. The column left the redoubt between 9 and 10:00 pm in two groups, leaving the 100 pack animals, the herd of cattle, and supplies. The troops were in luck because their redoubt overlooked their camp of May 15, which had been pitched along Pine Creek. Sentries would have been posted on the night of May 15 on the hill to the south and on the hill to the north, which had become the redoubt of May 17. It would have been following procedure for the "officer of the day" of May 15 to have climbed both hills to evaluate the terrain. I propose that the Indians made no attempt to secure the south hilltop since it was one-half mile from the May 17 redoubt and would not have offered a tactical position to stage attacks. Therefore, the officers knew that they would have a good chance to escape by climbing over the hill at night. Most important, the quarter moon[12] would have provided plenty of light for horses, enough for the troops to see near objects, but not enough light for the Indians encamped to the east and west to observe them. After descending the south hill, the troops turned east to retrace their steps along Ingossomen Creek. They reached Red Wolf Crossing the evening of May 18, a hard ride of nearly 90 miles! Upon reaching Fort Walla Walla, they secured the distinction of making the longest retreat in the history of the U. S. Army.

From the Army prospective, it seemed that the Indians had relaxed their vigil and not posted sentries on the southern hill, which was protected by a basalt rampart. From the Coeur d'Alene Indians' viewpoint, they won the spoils of battle without firing another shot. Moreover, they watched the soldiers retreat in disgrace. The Coeur d'Alene Indians did not share the booty. However, four months later, Wright made them return or pay for the supplies.

IV: Aftermath

A Brief Account of the Wright Campaign: Four months after the Battle of To-hots-nim-me, Colonel George Wright amassed 180 dragoons, 400 infantry soldiers, and 90 rifle brigade soldiers, all mounted, for a campaign against the Indian tribes that had defeated Steptoe. He also employed 200 mule skinners to drive a 400-mule pack train, extra horses, and supply wagons. Wright enlisted 30 Nez Pierce Indians, who were issued U.S. Army uniforms and placed under Mullan's command to serve as guides and combat soldiers.

On August 9, Wright's column of dragoons marched from Fort Walla Walla to the mouth of the Tucannon River. On August 25, the Indians swam the horses across the Snake River and the soldiers were ferried across on rafts. In his memoir, originally published in 1859, Lieutenant Lawrence Kip captured the feelings of this day when he referred to the Snake River as their *Rubicon*, the river in Roman Italy whose crossing proverbially signified passing the point of no return. After ascending the Snake River breaks and a 15 mile march, the army camped at present-day Hooper. A few days later, the army encountered Indians in the Four Lakes Region near Medical Lake. Riding bareback on painted Appaloosas, the Indians paraded on the plains, their faces adorned with paint, thrusting feathered lances and rifles. Their chiefs were wearing war bonnets. Kip quoted Lord Byron:

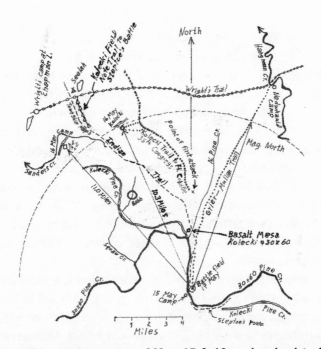

Pine Creek, Steptoe's camps of May 15 & 16 and redoubt of May 17

Pine, Sanders, Squaw, and Hangman Creeks were traced from a 30 x 60 minute topographic map of Rosalia. The Indian trail to Fort Colville is from three 1873 township maps that were scaled and positioned from section numbers onto the overlay. Wright's Trail from the Coeur d'Alene Mission (Cataldo) is from Mullan's Reconnaissance Map and was scaled to fit the topographic map by enlarging to 380 percent. The Kolecki Map of "Steptoe's Battle Field" was reduced 83 percent to fit the 30 x 60 topographic scale. All maps were aligned to true north. Pine Creek on the Kolecki Map was positioned to fit that of the 30 x 60 map. North Pine Creek (Grier's Route) and the ravine at "First Point of Attack" from the Kolecki Map exactly coincide to contours of the 30 x 60 map. The traditional site for the May 16 camp is at Squaw Creek and Babb Road. However, this location is too close to the "First Point of Attack" to fit the Kolecki Map; and neither a bluff nor a prairie bottom holding water in spring are present in the area of Babb Road. When the Kolecki May 16 camp site is rotated westerly 19° from the redoubt position of May 17, it lies only 0.7 miles from the rim of a bluff at Sanders Creek Valley. This site shows a "bottom" to the east. Kolecki's "Trail to Fort Colville" essentially superimposes on the Indian trail noted on 1873 township maps. Steptoe would have left Sanders Creek to march north between hills before being stopped by Chief Vincent about one mile south of Stubblefield Lake (Seelah). Steptoe's column then retreated one mile southwest to reach the rim of the bluff at Sanders Creek. On the morning of May 17, Steptoe rode east about one mile to regain the Colville Trail for his retreat route.

"By heavens! It was a glorious sight to see
The gay array of their wild chivalry."[13]

The Indians were showing their strength and rode openly since they thought they were out of range of the soldiers as during the Steptoe battle. However, the artillery had positioned its cannons on a high hill, and canon fire quickly dispersed the Indians into arroyos and pine groves. Dragoons charged and drove the warriors onto the Spokane Plains. The Indians' outdated Hudson's Bay rifles were no match against the army's new breech-loading Sharpes carbines, and the army pushed the Indians eastward toward the Spokane River. Fighting against superior firepower, the Indians attempted to gain range under the smoke of prairie fires, but the early morning easterly winds changed direction. The Indians melted into the mountains.

Wright rested his troops a few days along the Spokane River and then marched toward Coeur d'Alene Lake, plundering and burning Indian villages. In an act completely incomprehensible to native peoples, Wright ordered 840 horses shot. In his Congressional report, Mullan noted "that would teach the Indians a never-to-be-forgotten lesson." The trail from Coeur d'Alene Lake to the mission on the Coeur d'Alene River was narrow and dangerous, so the army abandoned its survey wagon and howitzer carriages. The column moved in single file.

The column stretched for 8 miles and required 4 hours to arrive at the mission. The troop companies bivouacked near the mission, making a powerful display of military might. Since the Coeur d'Alene Indians numbered only 450, Chief Vincent submitted to the harsh treaty imposed by Wright. On Sept 18, the army, with prisoners, hostages, and Coeur d'Alene guides, began its return march to Fort Walla Walla, following a trail south of Lake Coeur d'Alene to Camp Nedwhauld on Latah Creek. Here Wright offered death or unconditional surrender to the Spokane Indians, represented by Chiefs Garey and Polatkin. Considering that their winter supplies had been plundered, they surrendered. Malkapsi, humbled and whipped, rode into camp in order to save himself. Father Joset was present when Malkapsi appeared before Wright. Surprisingly, Wright allowed Malkapsi to sign the treaty.

Grier's Reconnaissance of the Steptoe Battle Field: From his Camp Nedwhauld on Lahtoo Creek (Latah Creek, Spokane County), Wright sent a detachment commanded by Major Grier to the Steptoe battlefield to collect the remains of those fallen and map the battlefield.

The detachment of three companies had returned with the remains of the men killed four months earlier on May 17, 1858. Kip had met the pack mules and helped the skinners unload the bones of Gaston, as well as the remains of Taylor, an Indian, and two of the dragoons. Kip remembered Gaston, his classmate at West Point, as a lively fellow, who anticipated a meaningful career. He thought of their gay parade uniforms and the spirit of brotherhood as he unloaded the *parfleche* that contained the bleached bones of his friend. He reminisced about Gaston, who had been fond of Shakespeare and Lord Byron, and how he had encouraged Kip to read *Henry the Fifth* and *Titus Andronicus*. Kip remembered that Gaston had told him on many occasions "tis more gallant to die in battle than spend your life confined to bed an' burdening our lov'd ones."

The sharp defile of the gulch fused with the rolling prairie as Kip acknowledged Gaston's wish: to be buried with his fallen comrades. "The fresh turf, and not the feverish bed"[14] suddenly spilled from Kip's lips. This quote from Lord Byron's *The Corsair Canton* had been one of Gaston's favorites and had been repeated often during their friendship. The fallen soldiers were buried at Fort Walla Walla.

This September, as I walked the valley of Latah Creek, I understood why it was a favorite Indian meeting place and why Wright decided to camp there. The tall grass would have provided good grazing and there was ample water. I imagined how the chatter of 1000 men had stilled when the packs were lifted from the sweaty mules. Only the shuffling of 800 horses and mules picketed about the valley would have disturbed the heavy, cool evening air. The canyon where Wright's Army had camped 150 years ago has changed little. It is a protected spot, safe from the winds scouring the hilltops. Standing in a gulch leading to Wright's camp, I imagined dragoons returning from the Steptoe Battlefield with the remains of the dead soldiers.

The Coeur d'Alene Indians crossed this canyon at opposing gulches and forded Latah Creek at a gravel bar when traveling west from Coeur d'Alene Lake to their spring camas grounds at Seelah. The Spokane Indians also used the ford when traveling south on a

Dr. John F. Randolph, from the Manring papers

trail now known as the Kentuck Trail. Thousands of years of footsteps, horse and horse-pulled travois travel had leveled the trail and smoothed the gravel bar. Pioneers named this place Smyth's Ford.

Hearing that Wright was merciful, some Palouse Indians also came into camp. Nevertheless, after hearing 15 minutes of testimony, Wright concluded that these Palouse Indians had been at the Battle of To-hots-nim-me, so he had them hung, despite the fact that they had permitted Steptoe's soldiers to escape from the redoubt and ride unhindered to the Snake River. The State of Idaho has retained the name of Hangman Creek as a reminder of this injustice, whereas the State of Washington has renamed it Latah Creek.

I am troubled by history as I look over this lovely valley where Wright hung seven Palouse Indians but pardoned Malkapsi. Had this been a miscarriage of Justice? Wright told the Indians that he would treat them fairly if they surrendered. However, this apparently didn't pertain to the Steptoe battle. As I stood at the granite monument anchoring the past to the present, images of garroted Indians shattered the tranquility of the valley. I was cold. I looked up through the canopy of cottonwoods that filtered the sunlight, preserving the frost-tipped grass. Flocks of geese winged south. It was late fall, Wright was out of supplies, his men were cold, and it was time to return to Fort Walla Walla.

V: Uncovering the Facts

In my quest to learn more about the Steptoe campaign of 1858, I rapidly discovered that I needed to understand the physical locations and relationships of exact spots where the story took place. Thus, my goals were to find the location of the Native American encampment of Seelah; of Steptoe's May 16 camp, which was the site of the second parley; of the "Trail to Fort Colville" printed on the Kolecki Steptoe Battlefield Map; and of the other trails where events took place. Then, I could walk where Vincent stopped Steptoe and where Father Joset had brokered the third parley. Finding these sites would give perspective to events that occurred 150 years ago. Consequently, my task was to place recognizable landmarks and trails noted by Kolecki onto modern maps. Since the Kolecki Field Note Maps were used to make those published in the 35th Congressional Record, I also retraced Wright's route, from Lake Coeur d'Alene to Latah Creek and then to Stubblefield Lake.

Indian Trails and Soldier Life on the Palouse Prairie: Donna M. Hanson's, *Frontier Duty: The Army in Northern Idaho, 1853-1876*, has been important for locating exact positions of many trails and sites. The original records are located in the National Archives, Washington, D.C. Hanson has faithfully transcribed field notes and maps of expeditions in the Palouse that were invaluable in reconstructing army life. I copied many maps and scaled them to fit 30 x 60 minute topography maps to locate the Lapway Trail and Kennedy Ford. I relied mainly on accounts and maps of A. A. Humphreys, Gustavus Sohon, P. M. Engel, Theodore Kolecki, John Mullan, J. L. White, D. Sherman, R. H. Fletcher, and George B. Sanford.

My Search for Seelah, Spring Camas Encampment: Several years ago, while visiting with Father Thomas Connolly at the DeSmet Mission in Idaho, I learned of the historic Indian encampment called Seelah and was surprised that its location had not been established. Seelah was first described by Mullan in his narration of the Wright campaign. In 1858, Coeur d'Alene lands stretched from Lake Coeur d'Alene south to the Palouse River, westward from the lake to Post Falls, then south to the Palouse River. Smallpox and cholera, introduced by the first explorers, decimated the Coeur d'Alene Nation; whose numbers dropped from 2,400 to 400 souls. The surviving families clung to their ancestral lands, and Seelah remained a major gathering place. My task was to follow the Coeur d'Alene Trail (Mullan Road) from the St. Joe River westward and thus locate Seelah.

I visited WSU's Holland Library in Pullman, which provided me with copies of original maps and the reports of Steptoe, Mullan, Gregg, Wright, and Joset published in the 35th Congressional Record. Each gave descriptions of trails, distances, and places. The problem was to put each on the same modern map.

The Wright campaign followed the Coeur d'Alene Indian Trail from Lake Chatcolet past Latah Creek to Chapman Lake. For the most part, Mullan indicated rivers, creeks, mountains, and lakes with such accuracy that they are readily identifiable on modern maps. In the following quotations taken from the 35th Congressional Record, Mullan's references to Indian roads and trails are in bold font.

After crossing the St. Joe River, Mullan wrote "at this point the **road forks**, one passing to the south to the camas ground of the Coeur d'Alenes; that to the north being the one we had concluded to follow. This **road**, leading through the bottom for seventy yards, ascended the steep slope of a pine-clad hill 1,500 feet high, gaining the summit of which we had a fine view on all sides for miles." The St. Joe River crossing is now covered by water and was located between Hidden and Chatcolet Lakes (both on Mullan's 1859 Map) at the site of the modern bike bridge. The southern road went to DeSmet through Minaloosa Valley. The northern road, which skirts Shoeffler Butte, is still present (it crosses Heyburn Road and is signed Mullan's Trail). Mullan continued: "Leaving the summit and descending this slope for half a mile . . . we gained an open prairie bottom . . . we encamped for the night, our march being only six miles." This camp was on Rock Creek about 2 miles east of Worley.

On September 22, Mullan wrote: "Following **this trail** for a distance of twenty-one miles to the Lahtoo or Nedwhauld creek, we encamped for the night, the **road** being over a rolling prairie." The next campsite, on September 26, was described by Mullan after leaving Latah Creek: "We reached a broad, **well beaten trail** . . . continued over a generally rolling prairie country, affording us an **excellent road**, and at a distance of 15 miles struck the Sil-cep-pow-wetsin creek." They camped about one mile north of Chapman Lake on Rock Creek. Mullan commented, "At a distance of 12 miles from our camp [from Latah Creek] we passed a broad prairie bottom, where were left standing the lodge poles of a large camp . . . which is called by the Indians 'See-lay'."

Kolecki noted the exact location of the Indian encampment in his field note maps (at the National Archives) with a cluster of 15 tepees. He also sketched a trail leading from the encampment and labeled it "trail to Steptoe's Battlefield." These were not transcribed onto the official army reconnaissance map published in the 35th Congress Records. Nevertheless, Mullan noted: "It was at this point that the main body of hostiles who attacked Steptoe were encamped, with their families." Mullan continued "This point looks out to the south upon a continuous line of prairie hills; while to the west, and four or five miles distant, was to be seen another line of hills, partially wooded on the slopes, with a belt of dense timber intervening, while far to the north and west, in the distance, were seen high, frowning, pine clad mountains." Mullan wrote that Seelah was at mile 12 from Latah Creek. Lieutenant Kip also recorded that the vacated Indian encampment of 34 lodges was by the side of a small cottonwood grove.

Armed with these details, I enlarged the trail from the Mullan Reconnaissance Map to overlay a 30 x 60 minute topographic map

(Rosalia) anchoring Wright's Nedwhauld and Chapman Lake campsites to the topo map. The route measures 13.5 miles, whereas Mullan recorded 15 miles. This difference of 10 percent could be expected with either Mullan's wheel-driven odometer or counting horse paces (his survey wagon had been burned at Coeur d'Alene). Thus, I reduced Mullan's 12-mile distance to Seelah to 11 miles, which places Seelah at Stubblefield Lake, which lies in a depression and corresponds to the 1 x 3 mile "bottom" shown on the Mullan map and at the edge of the rolling Palouse Prairie. An 1865 Department of Interior Washington Territorial Map of Roads and Trails shows a "Lake Silley," 11 miles west of Latah Creek and 2 miles east of a small lake (Chapman Lake).

Mullan noted that these "bottoms" held water in the spring and were dry in the fall, which explains why he did not show a lake. In addition, the Township map of 1873 (T22N,R42E), which was surveyed in October, does not indicate a lake at his location. Moreover, I have found Stubblefield Lake to be dry the last three falls. The land immediately surrounding Stubblefield Lake has been cultivated for years so the camas is gone. However, there remains a large camas field on the scrabble about one-quarter mile to the west of Stubblefield Lake. In addition, many small bottoms located in the Turnbull National Wildlife Refuge support camas fields to this day.

U. S. Musketoon   CAL. 70

Mullan also referred to a lake (Stubblefield) in his report of the Military Road: "our route of this date [July 14, 1859] while going east from the Sil-cep-pow-wetsin (Rock Creek) skirts the lake from which Colonel Steptoe retreated the day of his noted defeat at the hands of the . . . Indians." This statement implies that Steptoe had advanced to Stubblefield Lake. But, since neither Steptoe nor his officers reported the village of Seelah, I believe that the column was stopped in the hills a mile south of Seelah. A Map of Public Surveys in Washington Territory to accompany a Report of Surveyor-General made in 1865 shows the Mullan Trail, Chapman Lake, and a Lake Cilley, which is 2 miles east of Chapman Lake. Lake Cilley, Lake Silley, Stubblefield Lake, and Seelah refer to the same place.

A 1992 archaeological study of the Turnbull Refuge reports sites of Native American roasting pits, cave habitation and tool making.[15] Fitting Kip's description, there is a stand of pine, alder and cottonwoods about one-quarter mile west of Stubblefield Lake. This grove rings a 5-acre meadow with a rich stand of grass that would make an ideal protected campground. Father Connolly says that Native Americans only drank from living water and not standing water. In May, several springs feed into a small stream running north from this meadow. I visited this area with Father Connolly; Glenn Leitz, a local historian; and John Hartman and Raymond Brinkman from the Coeur d'Alene Tribal Headquarters in Plummer, Idaho. We tromped about for a few hours, but since this proposed campsite covers 20 acres, it would require field work to verify an encampment.

The Kolecki Field Note Maps and Notes: The original daily logbook containing the field note maps drawn by T. Kolecki, topographer on the Wright Campaign, is on file in the National Archives in Washington D.C. Kolecki used a scale of one-quarter inch to the mile. His topographical bearing sites were usually at recognizable land features. For example, the bends of Hangman Creek precisely show the location of Camp Nedwhauld and the campsite 15 miles to the west at Chapman Lake. Three miles east of Chapman Lake and on the Coeur d'Alene Indian Trail (Mullan Road), Kolecki indicated an Indian village with 15 inverted "v" letters and the "Trail to Steptoe Battlefield." Kip also noted that there were poles for 34 lodges at this location.

The trail from Hangman Creek west to Stubblefield Lake follows Bradshaw and Cheney-Spangle Roads. About 2 ½ miles east of Stubblefield Lake, the road bends around a prominent loess hill that is precisely located on the Kolecki Field Note Map. Kolecki also showed arrays of 30-foot diameter mounds of rocks that are still present, located north of the Cheney-Spangle Road between McDowell and Philleo Lake Roads; and he sketched the Philleo Lake bottom with surrounding hills.

My Search for the Army Redoubt of May 16: My father had given me Randall Johnson's *The Ordeal of the Steptoe Command*, which describes in a captivating manner the running battle and final redoubt of May 17 at Rosalia. However, Johnson's proposed site for the May 16 camp at Squaw Creek and Babb Road, which is widely accepted, does not fit the location described in the Kolecki Field Note Maps and Kolecki's published "Steptoe Battlefield Map." My starting point was to reduce the published Kolecki "Steptoe Battlefield Map" by 83 percent to overlay the Rosalia 30 x 60 minute topographical map. My goal was to anchor obvious landmarks noted on the 1858 maps to those on the modern map. However, there are significant discrepancies between Kolecki's Field Note Maps of the Steptoe Battlefield and the published map for the 35th Congressional Reports; and, the published map doesn't show many margin notations penciled on the Field Note Maps.

Kolecki penciled on his Field Note Map *Sketch of route to Col. Steptoe's battleground from camas prairie Creek [Latah Creek], Sept 24 & 25* "commencement of battlefield" at a point two miles north of the junction of North Pine Creek and Pine Creek at the junction of three ravines. Kolecki's three ravines exactly fit those of the 30 x 60 minute map. Kolecki carefully drew the trails from Pine Creek to North Pine Creek. He also noted a basalt mesa about one-half mile northeast of Pine Creek in the North Pine Creek valley, which forms a prominent landmark. Steptoe's soldiers crossed North Pine Creek about 400 yards east of the mesa to gain the first hill. Kolecki showed the retreat trail between two hills, where Gaston's and Gregg's companies killed the Indians.

Kolecki drew only 2 miles of the "trail on which Col Steptoe proceded [sic] and returned" on his Field Note Map. He also penciled "At a Lake 6 miles dist from the commencement of Battlefield the Col encamped and had the first interview with the Indians." This notation was not reproduced on the Congressional map. Nevertheless, on the published Congressional "Steptoe Battlefield Map," Kolecki drew a 3-mile trail that he labeled "Trail to Fort Colville." He also indicated "Col Steptoe's camp May 16th &17th 1858" to be 6.0 miles from "First point of attack" [this is the May 16th camp]. The field book notation, "Position of Indians on May 16th 1858," is reproduced on the published map. The published "Steptoe Battlefield Map" indicates a wetland [bottom] east of the May 16 camp, which could indicate the "sheet of water" described by Gregg.

Most importantly, Kolecki drew a mile-long, 50-foot high cliff adjacent to the May 16 camp on the Congressional Battlefield Map. Surprisingly, he did not draw this in his field note maps. Kolecki drew the route from Wright's camp on Latah Creek along the North Fork of Pine Creek and along Pine Creek to the redoubt site of May 17 with great accuracy. However, he did not sketch the west bend of Pine Creek on his Field Note Map as indicated on the Congressional Map! This would explain why the western, second bend of Pine Creek on the Congressional

Map is 7 miles too far north. I conclude that Kolecki did not ride the entire length of "the trail to Fort Colville" to Steptoe's camp of May 16. I surmise that Dr. John Randolph and/or Gregg, who were with Steptoe and had accompanied Mullan and Kolecki to the battleground, showed Kolecki the start of the trail to the May 16 campsite. I found neither a cliff nor a lake 3 miles northwest from the "first point of attack." However, there is a 50-foot-high, one-half-mile-long bluff forming the east wall of Sanders Creek valley and a spring lake that are 8.0 miles northwest of the "first point of attack." The Congressional Map shows the distance between the redoubt of May 17 (monument in Rosalia) and the Sanders Creek camp of Map 16 to be 10.3 miles, which is very close to the 11-mile distance on a modern map.

To help make the transition from the Kolecki maps to modern maps, I have relied on 1873 township maps that show many Indian trails and early wagon roads. Part of the Washington Territorial Road ran north from Rosalia to Plaza. At Plaza, three adjacent township maps show an Indian trail leading northwest for 10 miles. Consequently, I was able to anchor the northwest end of the "Trail to Steptoe Battlefield" at Stubblefield Lake and the southeast end at Plaza. It was on this trail between Sanders Creek and Plaza that the third parley brokered by Father Joset took place. From Plaza, at mile 8, the Indian trail turns north from Sanders Creek and follows a ravine between high hills. This location is at the end of Winslow Road (off Wells Road) and corresponds to Steptoe's description of "a dangerous place" and Gregg's account that Steptoe told him that they would have to "fight their way out." Gregg wrote that after retreating for about one mile they reached a "sheet of water," where they remained mounted for three hours before making camp. In his letter describing that night written shortly after the battle, Winder wrote that they rode about 2 miles before making camp of May 16. Even though there is no indication that Kolecki

DRAGOON PISTOL
MODEL 1855

rode the entire "Trail to Fort Colville," I propose that he did ride the 3 miles from Seelah to Steptoe's May 16 camp, because the published bearing of the cliff, the bottom that contained a spring "sheet of water," and the trail near Seelah fits Steptoe's description and are recognizable today. This valley and bluff at Sanders Creek is located in sections 32 & 33 in T22N,R42E and sections 4 & 5 in T21N,R42E.

In the preparation of the Military Reconnaissance Map of 1859 for the Congressional Record, topographers drew the Steptoe Battlefield Map onto the overall Military Reconnaissance Map. The transcribed distance between the camp of May 16 and redoubt of May 17 are shown to be only 6 miles apart. When transposed to the 30 x 60 map, this places the May 16 camp at Squaw Creek and Babb Road. This topographical error may explain why historians have placed the May 16 camp at Squaw Creek and Babb Road.

I have found neither a "bottom" that would hold spring runoff nor a bluff at the Babb Road site. By contrast, the 50-foot basalt bluff with a bearing 20° east along Sanders Creek visually matches the 50-foot bluff on Kolecki's "Steptoe Battlefield Map." The published battlefield map indicates that contour lines represent an elevation of 50 feet. East of the cliff, the land gradually rises for about 50 yards to a small loess hill that stands 25 feet above the basalt scrabble. Some 200 yards east of the loess hill is a "bottom" about one half mile in diameter surrounded by hills that match those on the Kolecki Map. In the spring this bottom is filled with water that could correspond to Gregg's "sheet of water." Today the depression is filled with invasive canary grass. There is a trail from the rim of the canyon down to Sanders Creek that may have been used by the soldiers to water their horses 150 years ago.

On May 16, 2008, I organized an expedition to Stubblefield Lake. I invited Father Connolly; Coeur d'Alene Indians Cliff, Frank, and Merle SiJohn; and John Hartman to travel some of the Coeur d'Alene Trail to Stubblefield Lake, to look over my proposed site of the ancient encampment of Seelah, and to visit the May 16 campsite used by Steptoe at Sanders Creek. I also invited Glenn Leitz, a local historian, and Richard Scheuerman, coauthor of *Renegade Tribe*. They all agreed that these sites were probably correct and that their proximity to one another would have explained why the Coeur d'Alene Indians had blocked the forward progress of the Steptoe command toward Fort Colville.

Evaluation of events leading to battle of 17 May, 1858

I propose that the 3.6 mile distance between Seelah and the May 16 army redoubt on the bluff above Sanders Creek convinced the Indians that the army would attack the next day. Seelah was not defensible, whereas the redoubt on top of the small loess hill overlooking the rim of a canyon to the west and a "sheet of water" to the east provided a defensible position. Steptoe may not have known of Seelah, which would explain his decision to encamp so near to the first parley. Chief Vincent probably concluded that Steptoe was on a war march because the troops had taken trails leading directly to his spring encampment at Seelah. The fact that the Indians permitted the soldiers to advance to within a mile or two of Seelah indicates that they preferred to avoid a battle, which would explain the second parley. Since the column had encamped early at 1:00 pm, and the troops had ridden only about 12 miles, Steptoe clearly could have continued his retreat. Thus, I posit that Steptoe hoped to salvage his mission to Fort Colville so he halted on a small loess hill that could be turned into a defensible redoubt. Moreover, Steptoe may well have been suffering from another attack of palsy, which he hoped would pass by morning.[16] Warriors pressed close but remained out of range. This was a standoff. At 6 p.m. the Chiefs rode to the encampment at Sanders Creek for a second parley. There is no account of what transpired; all we know is that it lasted three hours. I suggest that Steptoe accepted the resolve of the chiefs and assured Chief Vincent that he would continue his march to Fort Walla Walla the next day. Indians remained on the hilltops to protect their encampment at Seelah. At Seelah, Father Joset heard war drums from the hills surrounding the army redoubt. Had Steptoe been able to continue his retreat along the open Sanders Creek Valley he may have avoided a fight.

VI. CONCLUSIONS

A myriad of events ricocheting throughout the Columbia Plateau comprised the ingredients for war, which by chance, on May 16, 1858, intersected at a small spot in the Palouse where the Coeur D'Alene Indians intimidated U.S. soldiers to retreat near a place called Seelah. A running battle ensued the next day. However, the leadership of Colonel Steptoe and Chief Vincent prevailed to hold casualties to a minimum, allowing the soldiers to retreat to Fort Walla Walla. The Indians collected the spoils of victory. But the central question of the retreat from the redoubt beginning at nightfall on May 17 remains unanswered. Did the soldiers slip past the Indians guarding the southern front, or did the Coeur d'Alene Indians permit an orderly retreat in exchange for the supplies?

There are additional intriguing mysteries concerning the parleys that could shed light on the escape. Steptoe did not mention the first parley in his formal report although Gregg did. Gregg also wrote that only Steptoe rode from the May 16 encampment for the second parley. Why didn't Steptoe's officers attend the second parley? What did Steptoe and Vincent discuss for three hours? I conjecture that Vincent argued that Steptoe would have to leave his provisions to avoid a fight so that his warriors could claim victory without killing the troops. Steptoe's battle report in the 35th Congressional Record is only 2 pages long. It is also incomplete and required four follow-up letters of clarification. In his research on the Steptoe campaign, author B. F. Manring corresponded with Steptoe's sister, who wrote in 1911 that Steptoe had had an attack of palsy "during that Indian battle in Washington."[17] I posit that this attack of paralysis occurred during the second parley. Steptoe's affliction could explain why his report published in the 35th Congressional Record is short and seems to have been written from an observer's point of view and not a commanding officer's. Steptoe was well liked. Had his officers covered for him?

Three years after the battle, Dr. John F. Randolph, the surgeon attached to Steptoe's unit, wrote Steptoe's father that his son had suffered palsy during a return trip from Fort Vancouver to Fort Walla Walla in 1857.[18] Did Randolph inform Steptoe's commanding officer that Steptoe was medically unfit for command? Were there cover-ups in 1857 and 1858? We do not know.

---

[1]   To-hots-nim-me is a Nez Perce word for Pine Creek in the north Palouse Prairie where this encounter took place. Te-hots-nim-me and Tohotonimme are alternate spellings found on the monuments at Rosalia. The U.S. Army has adopted To-hots-nim-me as the official battle name, although Ingossomen is the Coeur d'Alene word for Pine Creek. Ingossomen (Hngwsumn) means "place where fiber for baskets is found," (Raymond Brinkman, Coeur d'Alene Linguist).

[2]   Colonel Steptoe's letters to his father and sister between 1841 and 1856, in B. F. Manring Papers, in the private collection of Greg Partch.

[3]   Steptoe letter on Jan 12, 1845 to his father.

[4]   For officer information: Cullum, George W. *Biographical Register of Graduates of the U.S. Military Academy, 1802-1867.* 3 Vols. New York: J. Miller, 1879.

[5]   Fort Walla Walla and Fort Vancouver Post Returns. "Returns from U.S. Military Posts 1800-1916." Roll 1343—Microscopy #617. National Archives, Washington D.C.

[6]   Steptoe letter, 27 Oct. 1856 to his sister. Manring Papers.

[7]   Steptoe letter, 27 Oct. 1856 to his sister.

---

[8]   Laurence Wright, Farmington, WA, relates that his Great Uncle Frank Leonard knew pioneer Henry Harlow, settler in 1870's, who had identified the Steptoe camp of 14 May.

[9]   Father T. Connolly, S. J., related information about Seelah from Coeur d'Alene oral traditions and Lucy Camille. She related that the camas grounds were at Hin-Ku-Ku-Mah-Wah (Water Lily Lake) and that Seelah meant Grandad. Also see ref. Burns, p. 214.

[10]   Ruby, R. H. and Brown, J. A. *The Cayuse Indians Imperial Tribesmen of Old Oregon.* Uni. Oklahoma Press. 1972.

[11]   Steptoe's sister wrote to B. Manring on May 2, 1911 that "Col. Steptoe's attack of Paralysis—in Washington—when that Indian fight took place—he was ignorant of the fact, as Dr. Randolph thought it best that he should not be informed." Manring Papers.

[12]   United States Naval Observatory (USNO). Moon phase display for the years 1800 through 2199. "Virtual Reality Phase of the Moon" for May 17, 1858, 20 hrs. PT.

[13]   Lawrence Kip. *Indian War in the Pacific Northwest.* University of Nebraska Press, p.56.

[14]   Kip. *Indian War,* p. 112.

[15]   Holstine, C., Galm, J. R. and R. Bruce. 1992. "A Study of Cultural Resources on Turnbull National Wildlife Refuge, Spokane County, Washington." *Eastern Washington University Reports in Archaeology and History,* 100-71.

[16]   Steptoe's sister wrote to B. Manring on May 2, 1911 that "Col. Steptoe's attack of Paralysis—in Washington—when that Indian fight took place—he was ignorant of the fact, as Dr. Randolph thought it best that he should not be informed," Manring Papers.

[17]   Steptoes's sister to Manring, May 2, 1911, Manring Papers.

[18]   John Randolph to Will Steptoe, M.D., April 8, 1861, Manring Papers.

References: Primary Sources

Gregg, D. McM. 1859. Report of The Secretary of War. 35th Congress, 2nd Session, Ex. Doc. No. 32, pp 65—67.

Hanson, Donna M. 2005. *Frontier Duty: The Army in Northern Idaho, 1853-1876.* Transcribed from the original records in the National Archives. Moscow: University of Idaho Library, 2005.

Joset, Father Joseph S.J. 1859. Report of The Secretary of War. 35th Congress, 2nd Session, Ex. Doc. No. 32, pp 42-48.

Kip, Lawrence. *Indian War in the Pacific Northwest: The Journal of Lieutenant Lawrence Kip.* Bison Books edition with Introduction by Clifford E. Trafzer, Lincoln: University of Nebraska Press, 1999. Originally published as: *Army life on the Pacific.* New York: Redfield, 1859.

Manring Papers, a collection assembled by B.F. Manring for the publication of his book and containing many original sources and photographs.

Mullan, John. 1859. Report of The Secretary of War. 35th Congress, 2nd Session, Ex. Doc. No. 32, pp 32-36, 48, 54, 59, 67-69.

Steptoe, Edward J. 1859. Report of The Secretary of War. 35th Congress, 2nd Session, Ex. Doc. No. 32, pp 60-65.

Stevens, Isaac I. *Report of Explorations for a Route for the Pacific Railroad near the Forty-Seventh and Forty-Ninth Parallels of North Latitude, from St. Paul to Puget Sound.* Washington D.C. 1855.

Wright, George. 1859. Report of The Secretary of War. 35th Congress, 2nd Session, Ex. Doc. No. 32, pp 55, 56, 58.

Secondary Sources

Brown, W.C. *The Indian Side of the Story.* Spokane: C. H. Hill Printing Co., 1961.

Burns, R. I. S.J. *the Jesuits and the Indian Wars of the Northwest.* Moscow: University of Idaho Press, 1966.

Emerson, S. "Steptoe (Tohotonimme) Battlefield Survey." *Archaeological and Historical Services Short Report 872*, E.W.U., 2006.

Gotfredson, Jon. "Fort Taylor and the Conquest of the Native Americans in the Inland Northwest." *Bunchgrass Historian* 28, no. 1(2002):12-18.

Johnson, Randall A. *The Ordeal of the Steptoe Command.* Spokane: R. A. Johnson, 1972.

Kowrach, Edward J., editor. *Saga of the Coeur d'Alene Indians: An Account of Chief Seltice.* Fairfield: Ye Galleon Press, 1999.

Leitz, Glenn. *Long Ago in the Northern Palouse: An Anthology of Pioneer People, Places and Events.* Spokane: Marquette Books. Spokane, 2005.

Manring, Benjamin F. *The Conquest of the Coeur D'Alenes, Spokanes, and Palouses.* Spokane: John W. Graham & Co.,1912.

Mueller, Marge and Ted Mueller. *Fire, Faults & Floods: A Road & Trail Guide exploring the origins of the Columbia River Basin.* Moscow: University of Idaho Press, 1997.

Ruby, R. H. and John A. Brown. *The Cayuse Indians Imperial Tribesmen of Old Oregon.* Norman: University of Oklahoma Press, 1972.

Trafzer, Clifford E. and Richard D. Scheuerman. *Renegade Tribe: The Palouse Indians and the Invasion of the Inland Pacific Northwest.* Pullman: W.S.U. Press, 1986.

Whitman County
Historical Society
Colfax, Washington

The *Bunchgrass Historian* is published by the Whitman Country Historical Society. Its purpose is to further interest in the rich past of Whitman County.

•

OFFICERS OF THE SOCIETY
2007 - 2008

President.............................Dan Leonard
Vice-President......................Dave Appel
Treasurer ....Cheryl Kammerzell
Secretary ....Edwin Garretson

•

MEMBERSHIP CATEGORIES

Basic $20.00
Family $40.00
Sustaining....................................$75.00
Patron .... $100.00 or more
Business .... $50.00 or more
Life.............................. $500.00 or more

Membership in the Whitman County Historical Society is tax deductible to the extent permitted by law.

BUNCHGRASS HISTORIAN
PUBLICATION COMMITTEE

Editor: Edwin Garretson
Editorial Ass't: Mary Jane Engh
                     Robert Luedeking
                     Kathy Meyer
Layout: Steven Watson
Membership: Sally Burkhart

•

•

SOCIETY ADDRESS
Whitman County Historical Society
P.O. Box 67, Colfax, WA 99111
e-mail: epgjr@wsu.edu
www.whitmancountyhistoricalsociety.org

•

SOCIETY PROPERTIES
Perkins House and Cabin, Colfax
Chatters Printing Museum, Palouse
The Archive, Pullman
Holy Trinity Chapel, Palouse

BACK COVER
Detail of the Redoubt of May 17, 1858, from a painting by Nona Hengen